Signs from Spirit
Journal

Other books by the author

The Awesomely Amazing Adventures of Cherry: Butterfly Buddies

Intuitive Symbols Coloring Book: Unlock your intuition through meditative coloring

The Spiritual Symbols Workbook: Create your personal dictionary of intuitive, psychic and metaphysical symbols

Led by Light: How to develop your intuitive mediumship abilities, Book One

Led by Light: A medium's guide to developing your intuitive and psychic senses, Book Two

Spirit Energy: Table tipping, trumpet voices, trance channeling and other phenomena of physical mediumship

Signs from Spirit Journal

Communicate with your
intuition, guides and loved ones
in Spirit through signs and
symbols in your everyday life

Rev. Joanna Bartlett

Cover images © Lilkar (Image ID: 20112248) and Vpublic (Image ID: 10264648) | Dreamstime.com

Library of Congress Control Number: 2018901748
ISBN: 978-1-945489-09-9

Alight Press LLC
2075 Charnelton St.
Eugene, OR 97405
www.alightpress.com

Printed in the United States of America

Contents

Contents

Signs from Spirit

Here's the good news: You're not off your rocker. Your loved ones and guides in Spirit really are trying to talk to you. They want to get your attention and get a message through to you.

When you're in non-physical form, connecting with someone here on Earth isn't as simple as picking up the phone to make a call or send a text. But there are still a variety of ways your guides, loved ones in Spirit, and even your own intuition can communicate with you, even if you're not a professional medium or psychic.

This introductory section explains what forms these signs from Spirit often take, why you receive them, who they're from and what your role is in the whole thing. Plus, it will explain how you can know if you're really getting information from loved ones and guides or if your imagination is making the whole thing up.

Knowing who's trying to get your attention and why, and what you're supposed to do about it, will give you a sense of being loved and supported by the very universe itself, helping you walk through your life with confidence and connection.

Forms signs can take

Communication from Spirit can show up in all sorts of forms. Here are some of the most common ones.

Feathers

If you find brightly-colored feathers or feathers from a special bird (e.g. a hawk or dove) in your path, on your doorstep or falling from the sky as you make your way through your day, Spirit may be trying to get your attention.

Some people believe a falling feather is a message from your angel, letting you know you're being guided and protected. Feathers may also be from a loved one in Spirit, to say hello or let you know they're nearby.

Feathers from Spirit are most often white, but can come in any color that birds do.

Cloud shapes

Ever look up into the sky and notice a cloud in a particular shape that somehow reminds you of a loved one in Spirit or seems to give you a message? The shapes these cloud forms most often take are angels and animals, but can be just about anything.

Spirit guides can come through in cloud forms with a sign that you're being cared for, you're on the right path, or to provide some kind of direction or message for you at that time in your life.

Coins

Pennies, nickels, dimes and quarters can all show up in odd places as a message from Spirit. We've all found pennies on the sidewalk and in parking lots that's just loose change that fell out of someone's pocket that they either didn't notice or didn't bother to pick up. But when you find a penny on your front doorstep, in your shoes when you put them on in the morning, or in other unlikely places, it's usually from Spirit.

Some people ask for pennies from heaven—or even dimes and quarters—and know that when they appear, it's a sign from their loved ones and guides in Spirit.

Animals

Certain animals, especially winged ones, like butterflies, can be a sign from Spirit. Butterflies signify transformation. Different birds often have a variety of meanings to people. And even outdoor cats, frogs, salamanders and other wild animals can be the bearer of a message for you.

Whoever you think of, see in your mind's eye, hear in your mind or feel in your heart, when you see these animals is who is trying to connect with you. You can also look up the symbolic meaning of different animals in books like *Animal Speak* by Ted Andrews.

Songs or music

When you turn on the radio or walk into a store or restaurant and the song that's playing strikes you in a certain way, that's Spirit trying to get your attention. The song or piece of music might have been a favorite song of a loved one in Spirit, or perhaps it was one of the tunes played at their funeral.

Another way messages can come through in songs is when the words of the song are meaningful to the situation you're in at that moment. The song may be connected with a loved one, or it may be a personal message for you, from your guides or intuition.

License plates

Messages on vehicle license plates can be significant numbers or names. In terms of numbers, they can be the year a loved one in Spirit was born, the year they died, or their favorite numbers.

Names, nicknames or initials can be spelled out either in a custom license plate or as part of a normal license. For example, a plate containing some combination of JYB7722 has my initials, birth year and one of my favorite numbers.

Bumper stickers, billboard signs and bus advertisements

Bumper stickers, billboard signs and bus advertisements can provide direct messages and advice, often with a dose of humor. If you've been concerned about something, if you've asked the universe or your loved ones in Spirit for advice, or if you're trying to make a decision, your answer may show up concretely and right in front of you as you're driving to or from work or on errands.

One of the reasons for this is that we often go into a bit of a meditative state while driving, allowing our intuitive mind and senses to open and be receptive to information from Spirit.

I often find these messages to be humorous in some way, especially when they're in the form of advertisements on buses or billboards.

Flowers

Not every flower you see will be connected to someone in Spirit. But when you notice a loved one's favorite flower and it stands out to you in some way, know and accept that they're touching in with you.

They may also be encouraging you to literally stop and smell the roses (or whatever flower)—to slow down and take a moment to connect with your inner self. We so often rush through our days, not really feeling what we're feeling, pushing it aside and distracting ourselves from what's really going on within us. Spirit and our loved ones want us to pause and take a breath now and then. They want us to enjoy the sweetness of life, even for a moment.

So when you notice a flower that brings someone in Spirit to your mind and heart, know that they're checking in with you and sending their love and support.

Phone calls

When you're no longer in physical form, you can't pick up the phone and call your loved ones still on Earth. But, sometimes, you can make their phone ring.

If you get a call from your loved one's phone—and their number or name shows up on your caller ID—it's them checking in with you. Sometimes your phone will ring only once and hang up. Sometimes it'll ring until you answer it, and find silence or static on the other end of the line. They can't actually speak to you as they don't have a human voice box anymore, but they are there. They just want to let you know they're around.

A client of mine told me that, after a reading with me, she got in her car and saw a missed call notification on her cell phone. It was from her late husband, who came through during the reading.

You might also get a call directly from Spirit. When I was in my early 20s, I struggled with depression and the complexities of becoming a fully-fledged adult. I remember one lonely Saturday afternoon when the winter light struggled to make its way into my apartment and I felt truly lost and despairing. I didn't know what I wanted exactly, but I didn't want to feel the way I was feeling. The kitchen knives began to look like a tempting solution as I sunk into a desperately sad place. I asked the universe for a sign that I was supposed to stick around on this Earth plane and that things would get better.

Minutes later, my phone rang. I looked at the caller ID and it showed: 000-000-0000. I answered the call and, while I can't explain exactly what happened, I knew that it was the universe answering me and letting me know I should hang in there.

Later that day, I asked again. "Are you sure?" The phone rang again with the same caller ID. I've always called those my calls from God. And these days I'm fully assured that the universe wants me here.

Repeated numbers

When you look at the time and notice repeated numbers, that's a sign from Spirit. Most often, these repeated numbers are 10:10, 11:11, 12:12, or 1:23, 2:34, 3:45, etc. You may also see repeated or increasing numbers throughout your day in other places, or the same number showing up over and over again.

These numbers can be a sign from your guides that you're on the right track or of a loved one checking in. They can be confirmation that something you've been considering doing is the right choice for you right now.

When these kinds of numbers show up in your life, notice what you were thinking about or feeling just before you saw them. If you were thinking about a new idea or path forward in your life, that's a clear sign from Spirit you should take it. If you were worrying about a situation in your life, it's a gentle hug from the universe, letting you know everything will work out OK and that Spirit is looking out for you.

Words in a book or article that catch your attention

When a piece of text jumps out at you, that's a sign you need to pay attention to those words and their meaning in relation to your life. Sometimes, as you look at the words, they'll seem extra bright or bold, or, as you read them, the voice in your head that reads as you read places extra emphasis on the words.

This is a message to you from your guides and loved ones to listen, pay attention and be open to how these words play into your life and its circumstances right now.

A book that falls off the shelf or lands open on a certain page

If you ever experience a book falling off a bookshelf or a book or magazine opening to a certain page—without any apparent help from physical forces—that's a loved one in Spirit working hard to get your attention. It can also be a guide bringing your attention to a specific passage or piece of information in the book or magazine.

Don't ignore these messages. It takes tremendous effort to make physical objects move when you're not in physical form.

Goosebumps and temperature changes

In my readings and intuitive sessions with clients, I know I've hit on something especially true and clear when I get covered with goosebumps. It's like a chill (a good one) goes through me and the energy feels crystalline clear.

When you get goosebumps around a thought, sudden knowing or situation, that's a sign you're connected with Spirit.

You may also experience sudden and unexplained temperature changes or the feeling of a draft or breeze when there isn't one. That's a loved one coming close to you. Their energy is on a different frequency than yours, which you experience as a cool temperature sensation.

Lights flickering and electronic phenomena

Some loved ones in Spirit love to play with electricity. They seem to have a knack for it and, in fact, find that it's an easier medium for them to communicate through than speech or other methods. It takes less energy for them to transmit their etheric energy into electrical energy and cause lights to flicker or appliances to come on. One of my clients experienced the TV in her bedroom being turned on repeatedly during the night until she realized it was her Dad saying hello and told him to cut it out so she could sleep.

Seeing shadows out of the corner of your eye

When people talk about seeing ghosts, most often they don't see a fully-formed, opaque image of a person. They see something translucent with less detail than you'd see in an ordinary human standing in front of you. And, sometimes, when your clairvoyant abilities are beginning to unfold and open up, what you first start to see when you see Spirit is more of a shadow or flicker out of the corner of your eye, in your peripheral vision.

When you look at it directly, it seems that there's nothing there. But you get the sense that there was something there, flitting about the edges of your vision. Trust yourself. That's Spirit.

Smells

Ever get a whiff of perfume, tobacco smoke or a loved one's favorite flower? These are all olfactory signs that your loved one in Spirit is saying hello to you.

You may be the only person who can smell the scent, or you may share the experience with someone else, either in the room with you or at the same time at another location. For instance, two sisters in two different towns, both thinking about their Dad at the same time might get a whiff of his cigarette smoke. That's him saying hello to both of his daughters.

Orbs in photos

Sometimes orbs and funny distortions in photographs are bits of dust, a thumb in the wrong place or your camera strap hanging in front of the camera lens. But other times, they're Spirit. Spirit orbs most often show up on photos taken during family gatherings: at weddings, birthday parties, graduation ceremonies and at the holidays.

Your loved ones still gather together with you and celebrate, even if they're not in physical form. You're never forgotten and always loved.

Dreams

Dreams of your loved ones in Spirit are often a form of communication from them. When you're asleep, you're in a receptive state, and your conscious mind is relaxed and open.

Some of our dreams of loved ones are regular, normal dreams where our subconscious works out the emotions and situations of our waking life, stores memories and rebalances itself. But some dreams really are loved ones visiting.

If the dream was particularly vivid or you wake up with a sense of emotional connection to your loved one, that means it was a real communication and not just your unconscious mind doing its thing.

Other signs

This isn't an exhaustive list of ways your loved ones and guides can communicate with you. Signs may come in other forms you don't expect.

For example, one day my youngest child, Benny, was getting ready for school and started complaining about all the leaves they were finding everywhere. It was autumn, but the leaves were turning up in unusual places: in the bathroom, in their bed, and under a shoe on a freshly-swept floor.

I smiled to myself and suggested that perhaps the leaves were a sign from someone in Spirit. Benny liked this idea and decided to take one of the leaves outside to put it back where it belonged and say thank you. As they looked for a special place in the garden, a tabby cat appeared out of the bushes. That made Benny smile, as they realized the leaves were coming from our cat, Hobbes, who died several years ago.

Who signs are from

Who are all these signs from? Signs from Spirit can be from a number of sources.

The most common are:

1. Your Spirit guides
2. Your higher self and intuition
3. Your loved ones in Spirit
4. Guardian angels

No matter who is sending you these signs, you can be assured and rest easy knowing that they are sending you your highest good.

Reasons for the signs you receive

Why do you get signs from Spirit friends, loved ones and guides?

There are a few reasons, which you've probably surmised in my explanation of the different forms signs can take. These are to *provide you confirmation, give you information and direction*, and to *offer you comfort and support.*

Confirmation

Many us go through life with a lot of questions about whether or not we're making the right decisions and taking the right road. Signs from Spirit can give you the confirmation you need to know that you're on the right track. This simple reassurance may be all you need to give you the confidence to keep moving forward with certainty in your step and joy in your heart, or at least a little less worry and self-doubt.

These signs often take the form of feathers, cloud shapes, coins, animals, flowers and repeated numbers.

Information and direction

Sometimes you may not quite know which way to go to begin with, let alone if you're on the right path. Signs from Spirit can give you quite specific instructions at times, or can point you in the right direction and give you continued messages of confirmation as you go along.

These often come in the form of song lyrics, a billboard sign, or a book that you feel called to read.

Comfort and support

Spirit loves you. Your loved ones in Spirit love you, no matter the kind of relationship you had with them while they were in physical bodies. If there's one thing that every person in Spirit I've connected with wants to let their loved ones here know is that they love them and they want them to feel that love.

Your loved ones in Spirit want you to know they haven't forgotten you. They'll never forget you and they'll always be available to you.

When you've lost someone dear to your heart, knowing they're still around can bring profound comfort. It can support you on your steps to healing from your loss and moving forward with your life.

Signs of comfort and support most often include, well, all of them. Any of the signs from Spirit you notice in your life are meant to lift you up, to help you know you're deeply loved, and that you're supported, always, on the path of your highest good.

Your role

So, what's your role in all of this? While you can't demand signs from your guides and loved ones, and you shouldn't go through your day searching for them everywhere, there are actually four things you can do to increase the likelihood you'll experience them.

These are:

1. Ask for and be open to signs

You don't have to do anything special, just be open to receiving signs from Spirit as you go about your day.

2. Notice signs

When something stands out to you, notice it without judgement.

3. Acknowledge the signs

After you've noticed a sign, allow yourself to consider that it might be a special sign for you from Spirit. Acknowledge who it might be from (that's whoever comes into your heart and mind at the time.) You can even say it out loud, "Hi, Mom!"

4. Express gratitude for them

Say thank you. When you think you're getting a sign from Spirit, give thanks for it. You don't even have to understand what it means at that point, just say thanks.

These four steps complete the energy circuit and makes it easier for signs and communication to happen more often.

The more you follow these steps of being open, noticing, acknowledging and expressing gratitude, the more you'll receive more and more signs in your daily life.

How you know it's real

One of the questions I'm asked most often in terms of symbols and signs from Spirit is how you can know if it's real or if it's your imagination. Not everything can be a sign from a Spirit guide, friend or loved one, surely?

And it's true that sometimes a coin on the ground simply fell out of someone's pocket, a billboard sign is just a clever advertisement, or the lights flicker because the bulb is about to burn out.

But then there are times where you have a feeling of connection with the Divine when a sign from Spirit shows up. **Trust that feeling.**

For instance, one of the symbols that my mother comes through is with a rose—either its scent, it's symbolic depiction or in physical form. I see dozens of roses every day. I have several rose bushes in my garden, they're planted all around my neighborhood and I have a silk arrangement on my piano. Most of the time, I notice them and think they're pretty, but nothing more. Every so often, though, the soft floral scent of roses will pass my nose when there are no roses nearby, or a particular rose will stand out to me and, at the same time, I'll think of my mum, feel her warmth or see her smile. Sometimes I hear her voice in my head. That's a true connection with Spirit.

Another way you know signs are from Spirit is the way they pop out at you from seemingly nowhere and draw your attention to them. This is especially true if you suddenly make a connection about what's going on in your life with the symbol for no apparent reason.

Ironically, it's at those times when you most doubt that you're connecting with Spirit because the thought or understanding is so out of the blue that you're truly connecting the clearest.

Finally, you can know a sign is from Spirit if it shows up over and over again. Spirit really wants you to get the message and will repeat it as many times as necessary in order for you to notice it and accept it. If you find yourself mulling over the same topic and seeing the same sign repeatedly when you think about it, that's Spirit trying really hard to get through. Listen!

This is a process of learning to trust yourself, your intuition and your inner knowing. The more you do it, the easier it gets. So, open your heart and allow yourself to feel the love and support that's so plentiful for you from Spirit.

What signs from Spirit have you experienced so far?

- ☐ Feathers
- ☐ Cloud shapes
- ☐ Coins
- ☐ Animals
- ☐ Songs or music
- ☐ License plates
- ☐ Bumper stickers, billboard signs and bus advertisements
- ☐ Flowers
- ☐ Phone calls
- ☐ Repeated numbers
- ☐ Words in books or articles
- ☐ A book that jumps out at you
- ☐ Goosebumps and temperature changes
- ☐ Lights flickering and electronic phenomenon
- ☐ Seeing shadows out the corner of your eye
- ☐ Smells
- ☐ Orbs in photos
- ☐ Dreams
- ☐ Other signs:

About Rev. Joanna Bartlett

Rev. Joanna Bartlett is an ordained Spiritualist minister and certified medium with the National Spiritualist Association of Churches, as well as an award-winning professional writer and author, and an intuitive medium and spiritual counselor.

She's the author of several books including the *Led by Light: How to develop your intuitive mediumship abilities* series, *The Spiritual Symbols Workbook*, *Intuitive Symbols Coloring Book*, and a kid's novel, *The Awesomely Amazing Adventures of Cherry: Butterfly Buddies*.

Born in England, she spent her middle school years in Barbados, then moved to the United States, living in Florida, South Carolina, North Carolina and Western New York. She now makes her home in Eugene, Oregon, with a passel of children (two pre-teens and two teenagers) and a lovely husband who does the laundry and rubs her feet.

When she's not helping clients and students tap into their own intuition and develop their ability to communicate with Spirit, Joanna enjoys cooking, gardening, spinning yarn and knitting, as well as brewing and fermenting tasty beverages in her kitchen. She's decided it's time for the family to get a dog, but needs a sign from the universe in order to convince her husband.

Learn more about Joanna at her websites, joannabartlett.com and alightintuition.com.

How to use this journal

When you write about your experiences and feelings, things can come into clearer focus and you gain a deeper understanding of yourself and your life. Use this journal as a way of accessing your inner knowing so you can live a richer, more authentic life.

Keeping track of these instances will give you a tangible sense of the synchronicities in your life and how the universe is looking out for you.

On the following pages, record your experiences about communication from Spirit, your guides and the universe, helping you along your path. Remember, the more you're open to receiving signs, the more likely you are to receive them and notice it when you do.

Follow the prompts, noting what the sign is that you receive along with the date and time. Then take a breath and center yourself and allow your inner voice to speak and give you information on who the sign is from, what it means and why it's showing up in your life right now.

Trust this process. Write down whatever comes. If it feels strange at first, know that it gets easier with time. Keep breathing, keep your heart open and trust in the process of opening up to the mystery of life.

Date: _____ Time: _____

Today I received this sign from Spirit:

_____

_____

_____

_____

_____

_____

When I check in with my intuition, I feel it means:

_____

_____

_____

_____

_____

_____

_____

I believe this sign is from:

_____

_____

_____

I sense this sign showed up in my life today because:

_____

_____

_____

_____

_____

Date: _____ Time: _____

Today I received this sign from Spirit:

_____

_____

_____

_____

_____

_____

When I check in with my intuition, I feel it means:

_____

_____

_____

_____

_____

_____

I believe this sign is from:

_____

_____

_____

I sense this sign showed up in my life today because:

_____

_____

_____

_____

Date: _____ Time: _____

Today I received this sign from Spirit:

_____

_____

_____

_____

_____

When I check in with my intuition, I feel it means:

_____

_____

_____

_____

_____

_____

I believe this sign is from:

_____

_____

I sense this sign showed up in my life today because:

_____

_____

_____

_____

Date: _____ Time: _____

Today I received this sign from Spirit:

_____

_____

_____

_____

_____

When I check in with my intuition, I feel it means:

_____

_____

_____

_____

_____

I believe this sign is from:

_____

_____

I sense this sign showed up in my life today because:

_____

_____

_____

_____

Date: _____ Time: _____

Today I received this sign from Spirit:

_____
_____
_____
_____
_____
_____

When I check in with my intuition, I feel it means:

_____
_____
_____
_____
_____
_____

I believe this sign is from:

_____
_____
_____

I sense this sign showed up in my life today because:

_____
_____
_____
_____
_____

Date: _____ Time: _____

Today I received this sign from Spirit:

_____

_____

_____

_____

_____

When I check in with my intuition, I feel it means:

_____

_____

_____

_____

_____

_____

I believe this sign is from:

_____

_____

I sense this sign showed up in my life today because:

_____

_____

_____

_____

Date: _____ Time: _____

Today I received this sign from Spirit:

_____

_____

_____

_____

_____

_____

When I check in with my intuition, I feel it means:

_____

_____

_____

_____

_____

_____

_____

I believe this sign is from:

_____

_____

_____

I sense this sign showed up in my life today because:

_____

_____

_____

_____

_____

Date: _____ Time: _____

Today I received this sign from Spirit:

_____
_____
_____
_____
_____

When I check in with my intuition, I feel it means:

_____
_____
_____
_____
_____
_____

I believe this sign is from:

_____
_____
_____

I sense this sign showed up in my life today because:

_____
_____
_____
_____

Date: _____ Time: _____

Today I received this sign from Spirit:

_____

_____

_____

_____

_____

When I check in with my intuition, I feel it means:

_____

_____

_____

_____

_____

_____

I believe this sign is from:

_____

_____

I sense this sign showed up in my life today because:

_____

_____

_____

_____

Date: _____ Time: _____

Today I received this sign from Spirit:

_____
_____
_____
_____
_____
_____

When I check in with my intuition, I feel it means:

_____
_____
_____
_____
_____
_____

I believe this sign is from:

_____
_____
_____

I sense this sign showed up in my life today because:

_____
_____
_____
_____

Date: _____ Time: _____

Today I received this sign from Spirit:

_____
_____
_____
_____
_____
_____

When I check in with my intuition, I feel it means:

_____
_____
_____
_____
_____
_____

I believe this sign is from:

_____
_____
_____

I sense this sign showed up in my life today because:

_____
_____
_____
_____
_____

Date: _____ Time: _____

Today I received this sign from Spirit:

_____
_____
_____
_____
_____

When I check in with my intuition, I feel it means:

_____
_____
_____
_____
_____
_____

I believe this sign is from:

_____
_____
_____

I sense this sign showed up in my life today because:

_____
_____
_____
_____

Date: _____ Time: _____

Today I received this sign from Spirit:

_____

_____

_____

_____

_____

When I check in with my intuition, I feel it means:

_____

_____

_____

_____

_____

_____

I believe this sign is from:

_____

_____

_____

I sense this sign showed up in my life today because:

_____

_____

_____

_____

_____

Date: _____ Time: _____

Today I received this sign from Spirit:

_____

_____

_____

_____

_____

When I check in with my intuition, I feel it means:

_____

_____

_____

_____

_____

_____

I believe this sign is from:

_____

_____

_____

I sense this sign showed up in my life today because:

_____

_____

_____

_____

Date: _____ Time: _____

Today I received this sign from Spirit:

_____
_____
_____
_____
_____
_____

When I check in with my intuition, I feel it means:

_____
_____
_____
_____
_____
_____

I believe this sign is from:

_____
_____
_____

I sense this sign showed up in my life today because:

_____
_____
_____
_____
_____

Date: _____ Time: _____

Today I received this sign from Spirit:

_____

_____

_____

_____

_____

When I check in with my intuition, I feel it means:

_____

_____

_____

_____

_____

_____

I believe this sign is from:

_____

_____

I sense this sign showed up in my life today because:

_____

_____

_____

_____

Date: _____ Time: _____

Today I received this sign from Spirit:

_____

_____

_____

_____

_____

_____

When I check in with my intuition, I feel it means:

_____

_____

_____

_____

_____

_____

_____

I believe this sign is from:

_____

_____

_____

I sense this sign showed up in my life today because:

_____

_____

_____

_____

_____

Date: _____ Time: _____

Today I received this sign from Spirit:

_____

_____

_____

_____

_____

When I check in with my intuition, I feel it means:

_____

_____

_____

_____

_____

_____

I believe this sign is from:

_____

_____

_____

I sense this sign showed up in my life today because:

_____

_____

_____

_____

Date: _____ Time: _____

Today I received this sign from Spirit:

_____

_____

_____

_____

_____

_____

When I check in with my intuition, I feel it means:

_____

_____

_____

_____

_____

_____

_____

I believe this sign is from:

_____

_____

_____

I sense this sign showed up in my life today because:

_____

_____

_____

_____

_____

Date: _____ Time: _____

Today I received this sign from Spirit:

_____
_____
_____
_____
_____
_____

When I check in with my intuition, I feel it means:

_____
_____
_____
_____
_____
_____

I believe this sign is from:

_____
_____
_____

I sense this sign showed up in my life today because:

_____
_____
_____
_____
_____

Date: _____ Time: _____

Today I received this sign from Spirit:

_____

_____

_____

_____

_____

When I check in with my intuition, I feel it means:

_____

_____

_____

_____

_____

_____

I believe this sign is from:

_____

_____

I sense this sign showed up in my life today because:

_____

_____

_____

_____

_____

Date: _____ Time: _____

Today I received this sign from Spirit:

_____

_____

_____

_____

_____

_____

When I check in with my intuition, I feel it means:

_____

_____

_____

_____

_____

_____

I believe this sign is from:

_____

_____

_____

I sense this sign showed up in my life today because:

_____

_____

_____

_____

Date: _____ Time: _____

Today I received this sign from Spirit:

_____

_____

_____

_____

_____

_____

When I check in with my intuition, I feel it means:

_____

_____

_____

_____

_____

_____

_____

I believe this sign is from:

_____

_____

_____

I sense this sign showed up in my life today because:

_____

_____

_____

_____

_____

Date: _____ Time: _____

Today I received this sign from Spirit:

_____
_____
_____
_____
_____

When I check in with my intuition, I feel it means:

_____
_____
_____
_____
_____
_____

I believe this sign is from:

_____
_____
_____

I sense this sign showed up in my life today because:

_____
_____
_____
_____

Date: _____ Time: _____

Today I received this sign from Spirit:

_____
_____
_____
_____
_____
_____

When I check in with my intuition, I feel it means:

_____
_____
_____
_____
_____
_____

I believe this sign is from:

_____
_____
_____

I sense this sign showed up in my life today because:

_____
_____
_____
_____
_____

Date: _____ Time: _____

Today I received this sign from Spirit:

_____

_____

_____

_____

_____

When I check in with my intuition, I feel it means:

_____

_____

_____

_____

_____

_____

I believe this sign is from:

_____

_____

_____

I sense this sign showed up in my life today because:

_____

_____

_____

_____

_____

Date: _____ Time: _____

Today I received this sign from Spirit:

_____

_____

_____

_____

_____

_____

When I check in with my intuition, I feel it means:

_____

_____

_____

_____

_____

_____

I believe this sign is from:

_____

_____

_____

I sense this sign showed up in my life today because:

_____

_____

_____

_____

_____

Date: _____ Time: _____

Today I received this sign from Spirit:

_____

_____

_____

_____

_____

When I check in with my intuition, I feel it means:

_____

_____

_____

_____

_____

_____

I believe this sign is from:

_____

_____

_____

I sense this sign showed up in my life today because:

_____

_____

_____

_____

Date: _____ Time: _____

Today I received this sign from Spirit:

_____

_____

_____

_____

_____

When I check in with my intuition, I feel it means:

_____

_____

_____

_____

_____

_____

I believe this sign is from:

_____

_____

I sense this sign showed up in my life today because:

_____

_____

_____

_____

Date: _____ Time: _____

Today I received this sign from Spirit:

_____

_____

_____

_____

_____

When I check in with my intuition, I feel it means:

_____

_____

_____

_____

_____

_____

I believe this sign is from:

_____

_____

I sense this sign showed up in my life today because:

_____

_____

_____

_____

Date: _____ Time: _____

Today I received this sign from Spirit:

_____

_____

_____

_____

_____

_____

When I check in with my intuition, I feel it means:

_____

_____

_____

_____

_____

_____

_____

I believe this sign is from:

_____

_____

_____

I sense this sign showed up in my life today because:

_____

_____

_____

_____

_____

Date: _____ Time: _____

Today I received this sign from Spirit:

_____

_____

_____

_____

_____

When I check in with my intuition, I feel it means:

_____

_____

_____

_____

_____

I believe this sign is from:

_____

_____

I sense this sign showed up in my life today because:

_____

_____

_____

_____

Date: _____ Time: _____

Today I received this sign from Spirit:

_____
_____
_____
_____
_____
_____

When I check in with my intuition, I feel it means:

_____
_____
_____
_____
_____
_____

I believe this sign is from:

_____
_____
_____

I sense this sign showed up in my life today because:

_____
_____
_____
_____
_____

Date: _____ Time: _____

Today I received this sign from Spirit:

_____

_____

_____

_____

_____

_____

When I check in with my intuition, I feel it means:

_____

_____

_____

_____

_____

_____

_____

I believe this sign is from:

_____

_____

_____

I sense this sign showed up in my life today because:

_____

_____

_____

_____

_____

Date: _____ Time: _____

Today I received this sign from Spirit:

_____

_____

_____

_____

_____

_____

When I check in with my intuition, I feel it means:

_____

_____

_____

_____

_____

_____

I believe this sign is from:

_____

_____

_____

I sense this sign showed up in my life today because:

_____

_____

_____

_____

_____

Date: _____ Time: _____

Today I received this sign from Spirit:

_____
_____
_____
_____
_____

When I check in with my intuition, I feel it means:

_____
_____
_____
_____
_____
_____

I believe this sign is from:

_____
_____
_____

I sense this sign showed up in my life today because:

_____
_____
_____
_____

Date: _____ Time: _____

Today I received this sign from Spirit:

_____

_____

_____

_____

_____

_____

When I check in with my intuition, I feel it means:

_____

_____

_____

_____

_____

_____

_____

I believe this sign is from:

_____

_____

_____

I sense this sign showed up in my life today because:

_____

_____

_____

_____

_____

Date: _____ Time: _____

Today I received this sign from Spirit:

_____

_____

_____

_____

_____

When I check in with my intuition, I feel it means:

_____

_____

_____

_____

_____

_____

I believe this sign is from:

_____

_____

_____

I sense this sign showed up in my life today because:

_____

_____

_____

_____

_____

Date: _____ Time: _____

Today I received this sign from Spirit:

_____

_____

_____

_____

_____

_____

When I check in with my intuition, I feel it means:

_____

_____

_____

_____

_____

_____

_____

I believe this sign is from:

_____

_____

_____

I sense this sign showed up in my life today because:

_____

_____

_____

_____

_____

Date: _____ Time: _____

Today I received this sign from Spirit:

_____

_____

_____

_____

_____

_____

When I check in with my intuition, I feel it means:

_____

_____

_____

_____

_____

_____

I believe this sign is from:

_____

_____

_____

I sense this sign showed up in my life today because:

_____

_____

_____

_____

_____

Date: _____ Time: _____

Today I received this sign from Spirit:

_____
_____
_____
_____
_____
_____

When I check in with my intuition, I feel it means:

_____
_____
_____
_____
_____
_____

I believe this sign is from:

_____
_____
_____

I sense this sign showed up in my life today because:

_____
_____
_____
_____
_____

Date: _____ Time: _____

Today I received this sign from Spirit:

_____

_____

_____

_____

_____

When I check in with my intuition, I feel it means:

_____

_____

_____

_____

_____

_____

I believe this sign is from:

_____

_____

_____

I sense this sign showed up in my life today because:

_____

_____

_____

_____

Date: _____ Time: _____

Today I received this sign from Spirit:

_____
_____
_____
_____
_____
_____

When I check in with my intuition, I feel it means:

_____
_____
_____
_____
_____
_____

I believe this sign is from:

_____
_____
_____

I sense this sign showed up in my life today because:

_____
_____
_____
_____
_____

Date: _____ Time: _____

Today I received this sign from Spirit:

_____
_____
_____
_____
_____

When I check in with my intuition, I feel it means:

_____
_____
_____
_____
_____
_____

I believe this sign is from:

_____
_____
_____

I sense this sign showed up in my life today because:

_____
_____
_____
_____

Date: _____ Time: _____

Today I received this sign from Spirit:

_____

_____

_____

_____

_____

_____

When I check in with my intuition, I feel it means:

_____

_____

_____

_____

_____

_____

_____

I believe this sign is from:

_____

_____

_____

I sense this sign showed up in my life today because:

_____

_____

_____

_____

_____

Date: _____ Time: _____

Today I received this sign from Spirit:

_____
_____
_____
_____
_____
_____

When I check in with my intuition, I feel it means:

_____
_____
_____
_____
_____
_____
_____

I believe this sign is from:

_____
_____
_____

I sense this sign showed up in my life today because:

_____
_____
_____
_____
_____

Date: _____ Time: _____

Today I received this sign from Spirit:

_____

_____

_____

_____

_____

_____

When I check in with my intuition, I feel it means:

_____

_____

_____

_____

_____

_____

_____

I believe this sign is from:

_____

_____

_____

I sense this sign showed up in my life today because:

_____

_____

_____

_____

_____

Date: _____ Time: _____

Today I received this sign from Spirit:

_____
_____
_____
_____
_____
_____

When I check in with my intuition, I feel it means:

_____
_____
_____
_____
_____
_____

I believe this sign is from:

_____
_____
_____

I sense this sign showed up in my life today because:

_____
_____
_____
_____
_____

Date: _____ Time: _____

Today I received this sign from Spirit:

_____
_____
_____
_____
_____

When I check in with my intuition, I feel it means:

_____
_____
_____
_____
_____
_____

I believe this sign is from:

_____
_____

I sense this sign showed up in my life today because:

_____
_____
_____
_____

Date: _____ Time: _____

Today I received this sign from Spirit:

_____
_____
_____
_____
_____

When I check in with my intuition, I feel it means:

_____
_____
_____
_____
_____
_____

I believe this sign is from:

_____
_____
_____

I sense this sign showed up in my life today because:

_____
_____
_____
_____
_____

Date: _____ Time: _____

Today I received this sign from Spirit:

_____

_____

_____

_____

_____

_____

When I check in with my intuition, I feel it means:

_____

_____

_____

_____

_____

_____

_____

I believe this sign is from:

_____

_____

_____

I sense this sign showed up in my life today because:

_____

_____

_____

_____

_____

Date: _____ Time: _____

Today I received this sign from Spirit:

_____

_____

_____

_____

_____

_____

When I check in with my intuition, I feel it means:

_____

_____

_____

_____

_____

_____

I believe this sign is from:

_____

_____

_____

I sense this sign showed up in my life today because:

_____

_____

_____

_____

Date: _____ Time: _____

Today I received this sign from Spirit:

_____
_____
_____
_____
_____
_____

When I check in with my intuition, I feel it means:

_____
_____
_____
_____
_____
_____
_____

I believe this sign is from:

_____
_____
_____

I sense this sign showed up in my life today because:

_____
_____
_____
_____
_____

Date: _____ Time: _____

Today I received this sign from Spirit:

_____

_____

_____

_____

_____

When I check in with my intuition, I feel it means:

_____

_____

_____

_____

_____

_____

I believe this sign is from:

_____

_____

_____

I sense this sign showed up in my life today because:

_____

_____

_____

_____

_____

Date: _____ Time: _____

Today I received this sign from Spirit:

_____

_____

_____

_____

_____

_____

When I check in with my intuition, I feel it means:

_____

_____

_____

_____

_____

_____

_____

I believe this sign is from:

_____

_____

_____

I sense this sign showed up in my life today because:

_____

_____

_____

_____

_____

Date: _____ Time: _____

Today I received this sign from Spirit:

_____
_____
_____
_____
_____

When I check in with my intuition, I feel it means:

_____
_____
_____
_____
_____
_____

I believe this sign is from:

_____
_____
_____

I sense this sign showed up in my life today because:

_____
_____
_____
_____

Date: _____ Time: _____

Today I received this sign from Spirit:

_____

_____

_____

_____

_____

When I check in with my intuition, I feel it means:

_____

_____

_____

_____

_____

I believe this sign is from:

_____

_____

I sense this sign showed up in my life today because:

_____

_____

_____

_____

Date: _____ Time: _____

Today I received this sign from Spirit:

_____

_____

_____

_____

_____

When I check in with my intuition, I feel it means:

_____

_____

_____

_____

_____

_____

I believe this sign is from:

_____

_____

_____

I sense this sign showed up in my life today because:

_____

_____

_____

_____

_____

Date: _____ Time: _____

Today I received this sign from Spirit:

_____

_____

_____

_____

_____

_____

When I check in with my intuition, I feel it means:

_____

_____

_____

_____

_____

_____

I believe this sign is from:

_____

_____

_____

I sense this sign showed up in my life today because:

_____

_____

_____

_____

_____

Date: _____ Time: _____

Today I received this sign from Spirit:

_____

_____

_____

_____

_____

_____

When I check in with my intuition, I feel it means:

_____

_____

_____

_____

_____

_____

_____

I believe this sign is from:

_____

_____

_____

I sense this sign showed up in my life today because:

_____

_____

_____

_____

_____

Date: _____ Time: _____

Today I received this sign from Spirit:

_____
_____
_____
_____
_____
_____

When I check in with my intuition, I feel it means:

_____
_____
_____
_____
_____
_____
_____

I believe this sign is from:

_____
_____
_____

I sense this sign showed up in my life today because:

_____
_____
_____
_____
_____

Date: _____ Time: _____

Today I received this sign from Spirit:

_____

_____

_____

_____

_____

When I check in with my intuition, I feel it means:

_____

_____

_____

_____

_____

I believe this sign is from:

_____

_____

I sense this sign showed up in my life today because:

_____

_____

_____

_____

Date: _____ Time: _____

Today I received this sign from Spirit:

_____

_____

_____

_____

_____

When I check in with my intuition, I feel it means:

_____

_____

_____

_____

_____

I believe this sign is from:

_____

_____

_____

I sense this sign showed up in my life today because:

_____

_____

_____

_____

_____

Date: _____ Time: _____

Today I received this sign from Spirit:

_____

_____

_____

_____

_____

When I check in with my intuition, I feel it means:

_____

_____

_____

_____

_____

_____

I believe this sign is from:

_____

_____

_____

I sense this sign showed up in my life today because:

_____

_____

_____

_____

Date: _____ Time: _____

Today I received this sign from Spirit:

_____

_____

_____

_____

_____

_____

When I check in with my intuition, I feel it means:

_____

_____

_____

_____

_____

_____

I believe this sign is from:

_____

_____

_____

I sense this sign showed up in my life today because:

_____

_____

_____

_____

_____

Date: _____ Time: _____

Today I received this sign from Spirit:

_____

_____

_____

_____

_____

_____

When I check in with my intuition, I feel it means:

_____

_____

_____

_____

_____

_____

_____

I believe this sign is from:

_____

_____

_____

I sense this sign showed up in my life today because:

_____

_____

_____

_____

_____

Date: _____ Time: _____

Today I received this sign from Spirit:

_____

_____

_____

_____

_____

When I check in with my intuition, I feel it means:

_____

_____

_____

_____

_____

_____

I believe this sign is from:

_____

_____

_____

I sense this sign showed up in my life today because:

_____

_____

_____

_____

_____

Date: _____ Time: _____

Today I received this sign from Spirit:

_____

_____

_____

_____

_____

_____

When I check in with my intuition, I feel it means:

_____

_____

_____

_____

_____

_____

I believe this sign is from:

_____

_____

_____

I sense this sign showed up in my life today because:

_____

_____

_____

_____

Date: _____ Time: _____

Today I received this sign from Spirit:

_____

_____

_____

_____

_____

When I check in with my intuition, I feel it means:

_____

_____

_____

_____

_____

_____

I believe this sign is from:

_____

_____

I sense this sign showed up in my life today because:

_____

_____

_____

_____

_____

Date: _____ Time: _____

Today I received this sign from Spirit:

_____

_____

_____

_____

_____

_____

When I check in with my intuition, I feel it means:

_____

_____

_____

_____

_____

_____

_____

I believe this sign is from:

_____

_____

_____

I sense this sign showed up in my life today because:

_____

_____

_____

_____

_____

Date: _____ Time: _____

Today I received this sign from Spirit:

_____
_____
_____
_____
_____
_____

When I check in with my intuition, I feel it means:

_____
_____
_____
_____
_____
_____
_____

I believe this sign is from:

_____
_____
_____

I sense this sign showed up in my life today because:

_____
_____
_____
_____
_____

Date: _____ Time: _____

Today I received this sign from Spirit:

_____
_____
_____
_____
_____
_____

When I check in with my intuition, I feel it means:

_____
_____
_____
_____
_____
_____
_____

I believe this sign is from:

_____
_____
_____

I sense this sign showed up in my life today because:

_____
_____
_____
_____
_____

Date: _____ Time: _____

Today I received this sign from Spirit:

_____

_____

_____

_____

_____

When I check in with my intuition, I feel it means:

_____

_____

_____

_____

_____

_____

I believe this sign is from:

_____

_____

I sense this sign showed up in my life today because:

_____

_____

_____

_____

_____

Date: _____ Time: _____

Today I received this sign from Spirit:

_____
_____
_____
_____
_____
_____

When I check in with my intuition, I feel it means:

_____
_____
_____
_____
_____
_____

I believe this sign is from:

_____
_____
_____

I sense this sign showed up in my life today because:

_____
_____
_____
_____

Date: _____ Time: _____

Today I received this sign from Spirit:

_____

_____

_____

_____

_____

_____

When I check in with my intuition, I feel it means:

_____

_____

_____

_____

_____

_____

_____

I believe this sign is from:

_____

_____

_____

I sense this sign showed up in my life today because:

_____

_____

_____

_____

_____

Date: _____ Time: _____

Today I received this sign from Spirit:

_____

_____

_____

_____

_____

_____

When I check in with my intuition, I feel it means:

_____

_____

_____

_____

_____

_____

I believe this sign is from:

_____

_____

_____

I sense this sign showed up in my life today because:

_____

_____

_____

_____

_____

Date: _____ Time: _____

Today I received this sign from Spirit:

_____
_____
_____
_____
_____
_____

When I check in with my intuition, I feel it means:

_____
_____
_____
_____
_____
_____

I believe this sign is from:

_____
_____
_____

I sense this sign showed up in my life today because:

_____
_____
_____
_____
_____

Date: _____ Time: _____

Today I received this sign from Spirit:

_____

_____

_____

_____

_____

_____

When I check in with my intuition, I feel it means:

_____

_____

_____

_____

_____

_____

_____

I believe this sign is from:

_____

_____

_____

I sense this sign showed up in my life today because:

_____

_____

_____

_____

Date: _____ Time: _____

Today I received this sign from Spirit:

_____
_____
_____
_____
_____
_____

When I check in with my intuition, I feel it means:

_____
_____
_____
_____
_____
_____
_____

I believe this sign is from:

_____
_____
_____

I sense this sign showed up in my life today because:

_____
_____
_____
_____
_____

Date: _____ Time: _____

Today I received this sign from Spirit:

_____

_____

_____

_____

_____

When I check in with my intuition, I feel it means:

_____

_____

_____

_____

_____

I believe this sign is from:

_____

_____

I sense this sign showed up in my life today because:

_____

_____

_____

_____

Date: _____ Time: _____

Today I received this sign from Spirit:

_____

_____

_____

_____

_____

_____

When I check in with my intuition, I feel it means:

_____

_____

_____

_____

_____

_____

_____

I believe this sign is from:

_____

_____

_____

I sense this sign showed up in my life today because:

_____

_____

_____

_____

_____

Date: _____ Time: _____

Today I received this sign from Spirit:

_____

_____

_____

_____

_____

When I check in with my intuition, I feel it means:

_____

_____

_____

_____

_____

_____

I believe this sign is from:

_____

_____

_____

I sense this sign showed up in my life today because:

_____

_____

_____

_____

_____

Date: _____ Time: _____

Today I received this sign from Spirit:

_____
_____
_____
_____
_____
_____

When I check in with my intuition, I feel it means:

_____
_____
_____
_____
_____
_____
_____

I believe this sign is from:

_____
_____
_____

I sense this sign showed up in my life today because:

_____
_____
_____
_____
_____

Date: _____ Time: _____

Today I received this sign from Spirit:

_____
_____
_____
_____
_____
_____

When I check in with my intuition, I feel it means:

_____
_____
_____
_____
_____
_____

I believe this sign is from:

_____
_____
_____

I sense this sign showed up in my life today because:

_____
_____
_____
_____

Date: _____ Time: _____

Today I received this sign from Spirit:

_____
_____
_____
_____
_____
_____

When I check in with my intuition, I feel it means:

_____
_____
_____
_____
_____
_____

I believe this sign is from:

_____
_____
_____

I sense this sign showed up in my life today because:

_____
_____
_____
_____
_____

Date: _____ Time: _____

Today I received this sign from Spirit:

_____

_____

_____

_____

_____

When I check in with my intuition, I feel it means:

_____

_____

_____

_____

_____

I believe this sign is from:

_____

_____

I sense this sign showed up in my life today because:

_____

_____

_____

_____

Date: _____ Time: _____

Today I received this sign from Spirit:

_____

_____

_____

_____

_____

_____

When I check in with my intuition, I feel it means:

_____

_____

_____

_____

_____

_____

_____

I believe this sign is from:

_____

_____

_____

I sense this sign showed up in my life today because:

_____

_____

_____

_____

_____

Date: _____ Time: _____

Today I received this sign from Spirit:

_____

_____

_____

_____

_____

When I check in with my intuition, I feel it means:

_____

_____

_____

_____

_____

_____

_____

I believe this sign is from:

_____

_____

_____

I sense this sign showed up in my life today because:

_____

_____

_____

_____

_____

Date: _____ Time: _____

Today I received this sign from Spirit:

_____
_____
_____
_____
_____
_____

When I check in with my intuition, I feel it means:

_____
_____
_____
_____
_____
_____
_____

I believe this sign is from:

_____
_____
_____

I sense this sign showed up in my life today because:

_____
_____
_____
_____
_____

Date: _____ Time: _____

Today I received this sign from Spirit:

_____

_____

_____

_____

_____

When I check in with my intuition, I feel it means:

_____

_____

_____

_____

_____

_____

I believe this sign is from:

_____

_____

I sense this sign showed up in my life today because:

_____

_____

_____

_____

Date: _____ Time: _____

Today I received this sign from Spirit:

_____

_____

_____

_____

_____

_____

When I check in with my intuition, I feel it means:

_____

_____

_____

_____

_____

_____

_____

I believe this sign is from:

_____

_____

_____

I sense this sign showed up in my life today because:

_____

_____

_____

_____

_____

Date: _____ Time: _____

Today I received this sign from Spirit:

_____

_____

_____

_____

_____

_____

When I check in with my intuition, I feel it means:

_____

_____

_____

_____

_____

_____

_____

I believe this sign is from:

_____

_____

_____

I sense this sign showed up in my life today because:

_____

_____

_____

_____

Date: _____ Time: _____

Today I received this sign from Spirit:

_____

_____

_____

_____

_____

_____

When I check in with my intuition, I feel it means:

_____

_____

_____

_____

_____

_____

I believe this sign is from:

_____

_____

_____

I sense this sign showed up in my life today because:

_____

_____

_____

_____

_____

Date: _____ Time: _____

Today I received this sign from Spirit:

_____

_____

_____

_____

_____

_____

When I check in with my intuition, I feel it means:

_____

_____

_____

_____

_____

_____

_____

I believe this sign is from:

_____

_____

_____

I sense this sign showed up in my life today because:

_____

_____

_____

_____

_____

Date: _____ Time: _____

Today I received this sign from Spirit:

_____
_____
_____
_____
_____
_____

When I check in with my intuition, I feel it means:

_____
_____
_____
_____
_____
_____

I believe this sign is from:

_____
_____
_____

I sense this sign showed up in my life today because:

_____
_____
_____
_____
_____

Date: _____ Time: _____

Today I received this sign from Spirit:

_____
_____
_____
_____
_____

When I check in with my intuition, I feel it means:

_____
_____
_____
_____
_____
_____
_____

I believe this sign is from:

_____
_____
_____

I sense this sign showed up in my life today because:

_____
_____
_____
_____

Date: _____ Time: _____

Today I received this sign from Spirit:

_____
_____
_____
_____
_____
_____

When I check in with my intuition, I feel it means:

_____
_____
_____
_____
_____
_____
_____

I believe this sign is from:

_____
_____
_____

I sense this sign showed up in my life today because:

_____
_____
_____
_____
_____

Date: _____ Time: _____

Today I received this sign from Spirit:

_____
_____
_____
_____
_____
_____

When I check in with my intuition, I feel it means:

_____
_____
_____
_____
_____
_____

I believe this sign is from:

_____
_____
_____

I sense this sign showed up in my life today because:

_____
_____
_____
_____

Date: _____ Time: _____

Today I received this sign from Spirit:

_____
_____
_____
_____
_____
_____

When I check in with my intuition, I feel it means:

_____
_____
_____
_____
_____
_____

I believe this sign is from:

_____
_____
_____

I sense this sign showed up in my life today because:

_____
_____
_____
_____
_____

Date: _____ Time: _____

Today I received this sign from Spirit:

_____
_____
_____
_____
_____

When I check in with my intuition, I feel it means:

_____
_____
_____
_____
_____
_____
_____

I believe this sign is from:

_____
_____
_____

I sense this sign showed up in my life today because:

_____
_____
_____
_____
_____

Date: _____ Time: _____

Today I received this sign from Spirit:

_____

_____

_____

_____

_____

_____

When I check in with my intuition, I feel it means:

_____

_____

_____

_____

_____

_____

_____

I believe this sign is from:

_____

_____

_____

I sense this sign showed up in my life today because:

_____

_____

_____

_____

_____

Date: _____ Time: _____

Today I received this sign from Spirit:

_____

_____

_____

_____

_____

_____

When I check in with my intuition, I feel it means:

_____

_____

_____

_____

_____

_____

I believe this sign is from:

_____

_____

_____

I sense this sign showed up in my life today because:

_____

_____

_____

_____

Date: _____ Time: _____

Today I received this sign from Spirit:

_____
_____
_____
_____
_____
_____

When I check in with my intuition, I feel it means:

_____
_____
_____
_____
_____
_____

I believe this sign is from:

_____
_____
_____

I sense this sign showed up in my life today because:

_____
_____
_____
_____
_____

Date: _____ Time: _____

Today I received this sign from Spirit:

_____

_____

_____

_____

_____

_____

When I check in with my intuition, I feel it means:

_____

_____

_____

_____

_____

_____

_____

I believe this sign is from:

_____

_____

_____

I sense this sign showed up in my life today because:

_____

_____

_____

_____

Date: _____ Time: _____

Today I received this sign from Spirit:

_____
_____
_____
_____
_____
_____

When I check in with my intuition, I feel it means:

_____
_____
_____
_____
_____
_____

I believe this sign is from:

_____
_____
_____

I sense this sign showed up in my life today because:

_____
_____
_____
_____
_____

Date: _____ Time: _____

Today I received this sign from Spirit:

_____

_____

_____

_____

_____

When I check in with my intuition, I feel it means:

_____

_____

_____

_____

_____

_____

I believe this sign is from:

_____

_____

I sense this sign showed up in my life today because:

_____

_____

_____

_____

Date: _____ Time: _____

Today I received this sign from Spirit:

_____

_____

_____

_____

_____

_____

When I check in with my intuition, I feel it means:

_____

_____

_____

_____

_____

_____

_____

I believe this sign is from:

_____

_____

_____

I sense this sign showed up in my life today because:

_____

_____

_____

_____

_____

Date: _____ Time: _____

Today I received this sign from Spirit:

_____
_____
_____
_____
_____

When I check in with my intuition, I feel it means:

_____
_____
_____
_____
_____
_____

I believe this sign is from:

_____
_____
_____

I sense this sign showed up in my life today because:

_____
_____
_____
_____

Date: _____ Time: _____

Today I received this sign from Spirit:

_____

_____

_____

_____

_____

_____

When I check in with my intuition, I feel it means:

_____

_____

_____

_____

_____

_____

_____

I believe this sign is from:

_____

_____

_____

I sense this sign showed up in my life today because:

_____

_____

_____

_____

_____

Date: _____ Time: _____

Today I received this sign from Spirit:

_____

_____

_____

_____

_____

When I check in with my intuition, I feel it means:

_____

_____

_____

_____

_____

_____

I believe this sign is from:

_____

_____

_____

I sense this sign showed up in my life today because:

_____

_____

_____

_____

CPSIA information can be obtained
at www.ICGtesting.com
Printed in the USA
FSHW02n0613080518
47792FS